Benji Goes to Texas

Book One in the Benji Series

Story and Illustrations by
Becky Uittenbogaard

Hog Press

Hog Press
an imprint of Culicidae Press®
PO Box 5069
Madison, WI 53705-5069
hogpress.com
editor@hogpress.com

Hog Press

BENJI GOES TO TEXAS

Copyright © 2025 by Becky Uittenbogaard

All rights reserved.

No part of this book may be reproduced in any form by any electronic or mechanized means (including photocopying, recording, or information storage and retrieval) without written permission, except in the case of brief quotations embodied in critical articles and reviews. For more information, please visit culicidaepress.com

ISBN: 978-1-68315-160-9

Our books may be purchased in bulk for promotional, educational or business use. Please contact your local bookseller or the Culicidae Press Sales Department at +1-352-215-7558 or by email at sales@culicidaepress.com

culicidaepress.bsky.social – facebook.com/culicidaepress
threads.net/@culicidaepress – instagram.com/culicidaepress
x.com/culicidaepress

Illustrations by Becky Uittenbogaard © 2025
Book layout and design by the author and polytekton © 2025

for Jeff — my best travel
buddy and friend

My name is Benji.
I am one year old.
I live on a farm with Jeff
and Becky in Iowa.
I am a Blue Heeler mixed breed.
I have a lot of energy, and I like
to herd and chase things.
My favorite thing to do is to chase tennis
balls that Jeff and Becky throw to me.
I also like to chase cars ... and chickens...

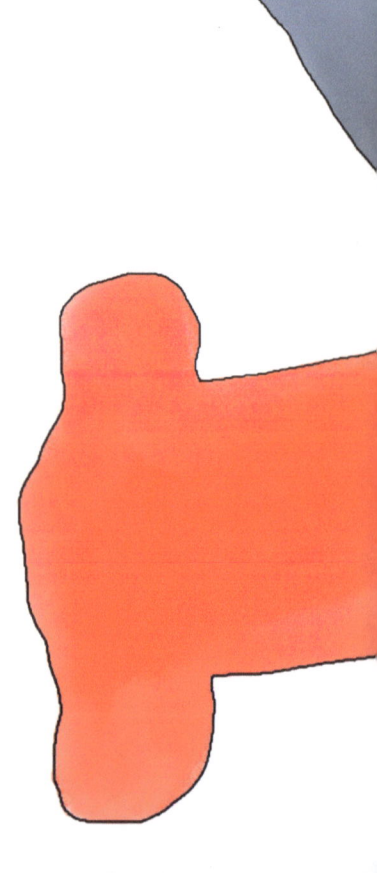

We are going on vacation, and our destination is Padre Island National Seashore in the state of Texas. You can keep track of where we are by using the map on the opposite page.

Becky thinks that, if we spend all this time together, I will become a better-behaved dog. Maybe I will learn not to chase cars ... and chickens...

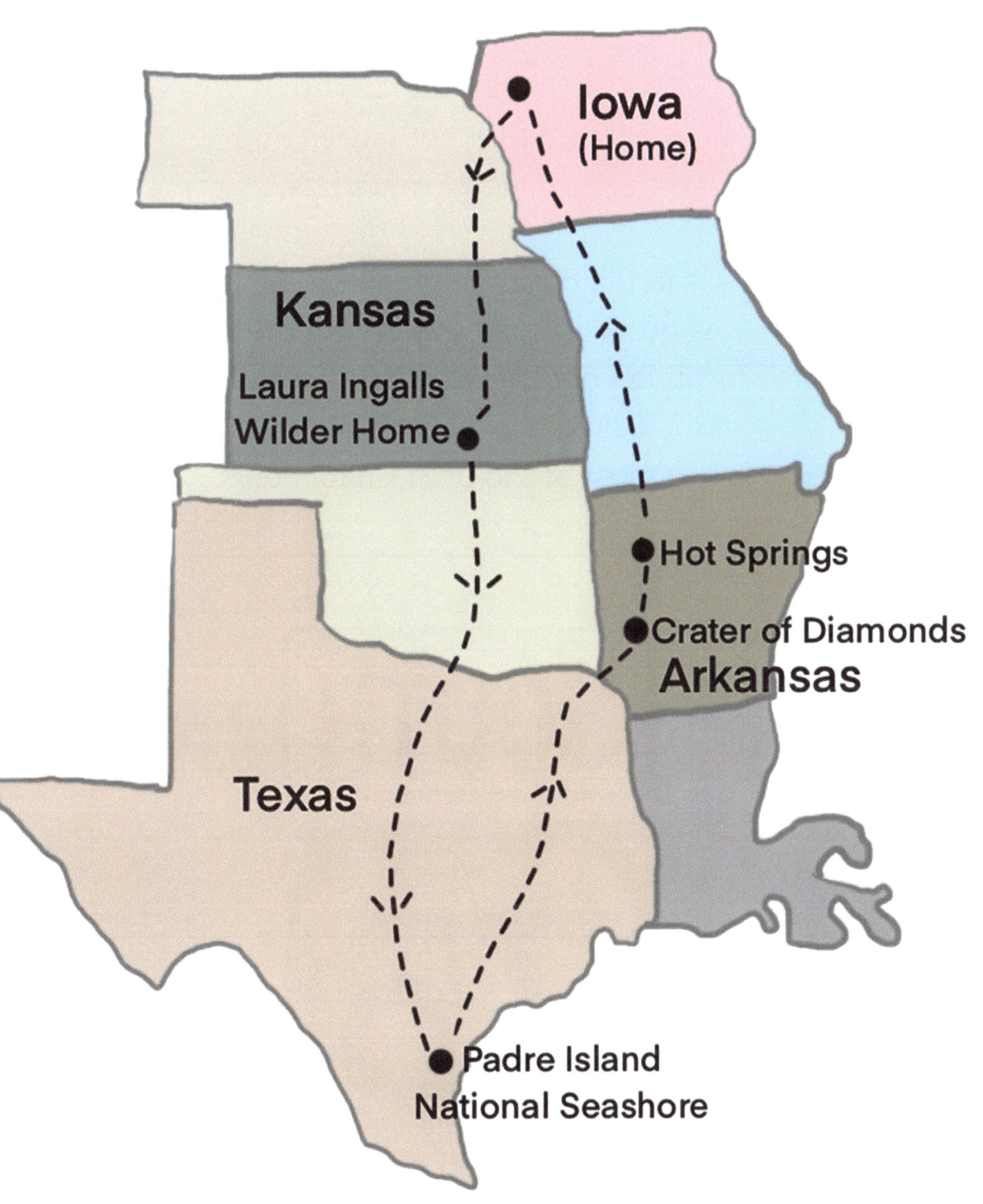

It was pretty scary starting out in the car on vacation. There were a lot of different noises and big semi-trucks around us.

I sat in the back on my pillow, but I was nervous and panted. But after a while I got used to riding in the car. I looked out the window a lot, but most of the time I napped.

The first night we camped in Kansas, and we all slept in the car! Jeff and Becky slept in the back of the car, and I slept on the passenger seat in the front. In the morning, I had coffee with Jeff.

That morning we stopped for another coffee and a lemon bar at a coffee shop. I didn't get any of the lemon bar, but I did bark at some of the customers — even though Becky told me not to.

Later that day we stopped at the Laura Ingalls Wilder homestead near Independence, Kansas.

There were donkeys in a pen there. Jeff said not to bark at the donkeys, but I barked at them anyway.

"Remember well, and bear in mind, a constant friend is hard to find."
Laura Ingalls Wilder

I met Penny, the basset hound, and her owners at a campground in Texas. Becky said to be nice to Penny, but I barked at her, which isn't the best way to make friends.

A couple of times Jeff threw my ball by a lake, and I ran to get it. It was so much fun! I am pretty sure this was my favorite part of the trip!

We did make it to Padre Island National Seashore. We walked on the seashore, and we drove our car on the beach!

I got sand on my nose!

I saw seagulls.

I also saw waves. Waves are a little scary because they come at your paws and try to grab you. I learned to jump over them.

We took several family photos at the seashore. Which one do you like best?

At Port Aransas we saw big ocean liner ships coming into port. One of them blew a loud horn. I was pretty scared, but Jeff didn't look scared, so I decided not to be scared either.

We camped near the seashore for a few days. I love to sleep in the tent at night. Sometimes I would sneakily put my paw or my head on Becky in the middle of the night.

Jeff made us eggs and spam for breakfast!

We decided to stay in a hotel for a while. We took our suitcases up to our room, and then we relaxed.

One of my favorite ways to relax is to take one of Becky's socks. They smell just like her, and it is so comforting to have a sock by me.

One day we went and got donuts, and Jeff gave me some of his donut!

We also went to a dog park. I learned how to play on some of the toys there.

We visited the Fulton Mansion. Dogs were not allowed inside, but I did get to sniff things outside of the mansion.

When we left the mansion, we stopped to buy a snow cone!

We also went to the Texas State Aquarium. I stayed in the car which was in the shade under a big bridge. Jeff and Becky kept coming out to check on me.

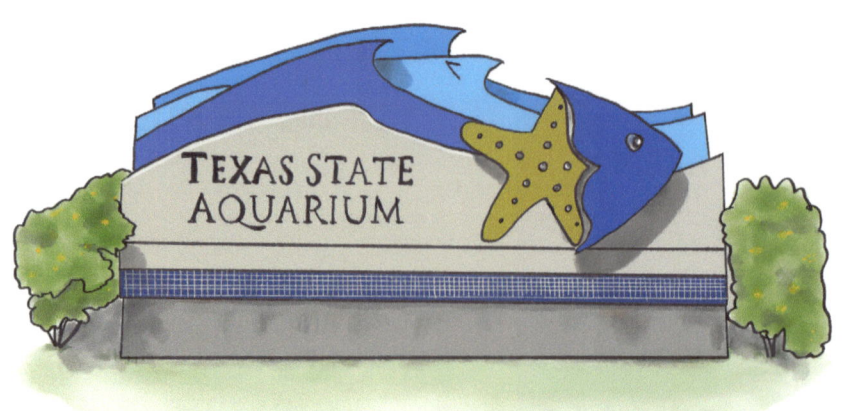

On the drive back to our hotel, they told me all about the dolphin show and the flamingoes they saw.

I would love to chase flamingoes!

We finally started the long drive back home to Iowa. On the way, we stopped at Crater of Diamonds State Park in Arkansas and went diamond hunting! The park is a big dirt patch with people all over looking for and digging for diamonds.

Becky kept telling me to look for diamonds, but I was too busy watching (and barking) at all the people and dogs that were there.

Jeff used sluice boxes with water to pan for diamonds. Becky looked for diamonds on the surface of the ground. We didn't find any diamonds.

We stopped in Hot Springs, Arkansas for a few days. I got to go hiking in the woods. We hiked five miles!

We saw the historic bath houses.

Jeff tried to dip his feet into the hot springs, but it was way too hot! It was 134 degrees!

We finally made it home! It was a fun trip, but I really like being back home on the farm. Becky thinks that I learned a lot of new things on the trip and that I have become a little bit better behaved. I still like to chase cars and chickens, though.

www.ingramcontent.com/pod-product-compliance
Lightning Source LLC
Chambersburg PA
CBHW041527070526
44585CB00003B/113